Welcome *and other poems*

The poems in this, the first collection of Geoffrey
Summerfield's poetry to be published, are written in styles
as varied as their subject matter. He is fascinated by words
and has a masterly way with them, entertaining with an
ingenious pun or an unusual juxtaposition of unlikely
notions, but at the same time stirring the imagination with
a startlingly simple statement or a flash of perception that
makes us see the familiar in a quite different way. This is
a stimulating collection, easy to read and easier to enjoy.

Geoffrey Summerfield is best known as the editor of
Penguin Educational's famous *Voices* series, still widely used
in schools. He now lives and teaches in New York.

Welcome *and other poems*

GEOFFREY SUMMERFIELD

Illustrations by Karen Usborne

ANDRE DEUTSCH

To Joyce Oldmeadow, of Dromkeen

First published in 1983 by
André Deutsch Limited
105 Great Russell Street London WC1

Photoset by Rowland Phototypesetting Limited
Bury St Edmunds, Suffolk.
Printed in Great Britain by St Edmundsbury Press,
Bury St Edmunds, Suffolk

ISBN 0 233 97528 4

First published in the United States of America 1983
Library of Congress Number 82-073988

Contents

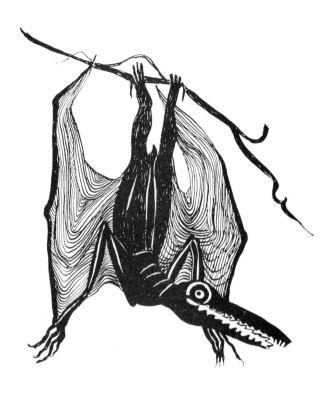

Welcome!

Come in! Come in! And close the door.
I don't think you've been here before?
Sit yourself down. I think there's room.
Here, take this chair. I'll move the broom.
I hope you won't mind all this mess –
The snakes and general untidiness.
I was looking for a rhyme for axolotl.
Like some cider? Here, take the bottle.
And I still need a rhyme for pterodactyl.
My wife's out at work. She'll not be back till
Six or seven. Even eight, if she's late.
I'm sorry the room is in such a state.
Now where were we? Oh dear, ah yes,
I'm sorry the house is such a mess.

Yesterday the House was Full of Flies

One went spinning down the plughole,
Clinging to a tea-leaf.
Two pestered the dog. He snapped, and caught
   them.
He was as surprised as the flies.
Three sat all day on a fruit-loaf,
Disguised as currants.
Four zizzed in a spider's web,
Until the spider woke up.
Five chased each other round a lamp-shade
Until they were giddy.
Six padded up and down the windows,
And still can't fathom glass.
Seven sat on the warm electric kettle,
Until I switched it on.
Eight stuck to reading all about glue
In the fly-paper.
Nine played on a broken fly-swatter,
Laughing themselves silly.
Ten walked all over the mirror,
Admiring their stomachs.
Eleven pestered each other, trying to bark,
Doing an imitation of a dog-fight.
Twelve went supersonic into the window,
Knocked themselves out.
And hundreds just sat for hours,
Twiddling their legs.
I folded a paper, killed one,
And a thousand more came to its funeral.

A Visitor

'What is that shadow?
There in the fireplace.
Surely it's a mouse.
Can't you see its face?'

    'There's something there, agreed.
    But it can't be a mouse.
    No way it could get in.
    There's no hole in the house.'

'Don't move. Sit still.
Its ears are sticking out.
It's in the corner, there.
It's a mouse, without a doubt.'

    'Well, what a surprise.
    You could knock me down with a feather.
    It must have come in from the cold.
    It doesn't like the weather!'

We watched for half an hour
But didn't see it disappear.
We've no idea where it went,
And haven't seen it for a year.

In and out of our lives
The creatures come and go,
Amusing us for free.
I wonder if they know.

The Defence

A silent murderer,
A kestrel came today,
Canny marauder
In search of prey.

He scanned the ground for signs,
Hovered on the lifting air,
His claws poised ready to snatch
Some victim off to his lair.

But swallows gathered fast,
Closed in from all around,
Sounding a shrill alarm,
Filling the sky with furious sound.

They soared into the sky,
And peeled off to attack,
Jabbing with dagger beak and needling cry
To drive the killer back.

The kestrel wavered once,
Then, like a useless glove
Thrown down, he tumbled on the wind
And fled from the birds above.

And we who sat and watched,
We too had been afeared,
Had held our bated breath.
But now we stood up and cheered!

9

Season of Sport

The pheasant glows and gleams
In his finest autumn plumes.

He is a moving feast of flame,
And yesterday the cornfields curtained him.

He walked through secrecy, invisible,
Now he stalks tall, stilted in the stubble.

Any minute now, guns will bark and snap,
And hounds will trigger themselves to grip.

You will pass a scuffed disarray of chaff,
A scrabble of feathers, bloodstained stiff.

March

Like snow, feathers drifted afloat
Where the hungry fox had sprung
And caught the chicken by the throat:

A mess of broken tail and wing
And a light flurry of white
Caught in wind's wild moaning.

And August

We found a nest under a curving tile,
Tucked in, safe from all weathers.
Grass and leaves cupped a cosy hole.

Lining the nest was a downy bed
Of soft white feathers:
A brood had come to life in the gift of the dead.

Reflections

'When winds are still,
See me in the mill
Pond,' says the willow.

'But when winds hurry,
See me all flurry
And blurry.'

'Like a black bow and arrow
In the water see me follow,'
Says the swallow.

'When gnats billow,
Fat and fallow,
See me swallow!'

Not a Word

Our gerbil
Isn't verbal.

Not a word —
It's absurd!

No verbs, no nouns,
Not even pronouns.

Sometimes he squeaks
But he never speaks.

He spends all morning
Just yawning.

Then he goes to sleep —
Not a peep.

He nibbles wheat on stalks
But he never talks.

It's a good life:
No trouble or strife.

He's not dumb.
But he is mum.

Cats

Old Tom

Old Tom is tabby
With some grey on his nose.
Old Tom is shabby
And wears old clothes.

Old Tom is crabby –
He growls and he bites.
Old Tom is scabby,
With scars of old fights.

His tongue's like a grater
His ears are both ragged.
His tail's like a taper
And his teeth are all jagged.

Most of the day
He takes forty winks.
If you ask him to play
He just growls, yawns, and blinks.

Why Stroke A Cat?

My purrpose, surr,
Is to make pusspurr.

Catrobat

Tiptops the wall,
Leaps down.
Turns alley-gaiter.
Fakes a stroll.
Finds cat-hole,
Whiskers-wide,
Slips inside.

Happy Cat

Flix ear;
Lix fur;
Pix lice:
Felix.

Cat and Cactus

Snoopy, our loopy old cat, tired of licking kittens
Into shape in our back kitchen,
Slunk out of the house, sniffing the track
Of a canny mouse, and snuck into the greenhouse
(Mostly quite white) of our neighbours, the
    Greenfingers
(Who were really quite pink, I think).

There she met a three foot cactus, Mexican,
All spick and span (and mostly greens and fawns)
Standing in sand, waving six arms, each with a hand
All prickles, sharp spikes, and thorns.

'Stop!' the cactus seemed to shout, holding out
Forbidding arms, just like a traffic-cop,
A spiky guardian of ripening tomatoes (turning
    reddy).
Snoopy sidled past but spikes of cactus
Caught her short and very sharp, in her breadbasket.
It was a shock. With temper now prickly,
She growled and quickly snapped, 'You scratch my
    back,
And I'll scratch yours, you green thing!'

She thumped and poked that static cactus,
Till it jangled like a broken harp.
Then put her foot in it, with claws razor-sharp,
And clawed and pawed, her hackles rising.
She started prising at its shallow root,
Rooting for that mouse (which was sandy brown)

Down and down she scratched and dug,
Until the cactus root came away at the foot,
Unseated by her catty feat, and for her feline honour,

Three feet of cactus fell about and on her
And six floppy arms, striking first her face,
Fell about her back in a shocking embrace.

Snoopy was loaded! And goaded into flight
She snarled and beat a hasty retreat, uptight,
With that green guardian riding astride her back.
She ran amok, fled down the garden, over the tubs,
Deep into the shrubs, with her green rider astride
    her.

'Look! Our cactus!' shortsighted Greenfinger cried.
'It's leaving home! Did you ever see such a sight?
Must be on the run, in pursuit of the sun!'

Mrs. Greenfinger blew her nose, loud and furious,
Spraying a rose, then turned to her mate,
With a bit of a smile and a bit of a frown.
'A funny business, fate. Yes, very curious.
But I had a hunch just before lunch
That that plant has never settled down.
I can't say I'm sorry. We never did really click,
Me and that truculent succulent. Homesick,
Most likely. I suppose it'll go, back to Mexico.'

The Rescue
For Jann, and everybody at Looking Glass School

Early one quiet morning there it was —
A hedgehog, clenched as small as a baby's fist,
Clenched like an angry fist with sudden fright:
A car had smashed to smithereens his mate.

Dazed, we went sniffing at the blood and bits.
We stopped to offer what we could.
He twitched and rolled his startled self
Into his private prickly little world.

Questions like pin-pricks darted at our minds,
And scattered all at once in all directions:
Should we then rescue him? Leave him alone?
Where were the parents? Had he been weaned?

That fragile smidgeon surely needed us —
Traffic would roar again and run him down.
Where was the food for such a helpless mouth?
We took him up and carried him back home,

Built him a nest of crisp dry grass and leaves,
And straightway he shuffled in, glad of the dark.
We placed a saucer full of bread and milk.
He came out and paddled, sniffed, and drank.

For weeks he seemed to like his B. and B.
Each dusk he lapped and stretched, gobbled and
    sniffed.
Then he just slipped away, into thin air,
And every day we ask 'Is he still alive?'

'Where is he wandering? What has he found?
Will he ever come snuffling back to us?
Will winter freeze too hard for him?'
And still we look each day for his return.

Old Goat
For Lizzie and Race Newton

Billy, the bully-boy billy-goat,
Has a beard that's two feet long,
A jet-black shining rug of a coat
And a pungent sweet-sour pong.

His eyes are dark brown aniseed
With a window of black in the middle.
He looks quite mad when he's ready to feed
And complains like an old broken fiddle.

Inside his pen he thumps and struts,
And gives each wall a nudge,
Thrusts at the door, and kicks and butts,
And if ever that door should budge

I'd run like greased lightning for many a mile,
Cross the stream with one frantic bound,
I'd leap high over every gate and stile:
My feet wouldn't even touch the ground!

But if he ever caught me — and Heaven forbid! —
He'd lead me a crazy dance.
He's been eyeing my trousers since only a kid
And my legs, like my breath, would end up in short
    pants!

Snapshots

Blackberry Song

The bramble bush is full of noises.
The blackberry flowers are testing their voices?
Making rich dark music, hour after hour,
The bees are bumbling at the ears of each flower.

Amazing

The centipede moves at breakneck speed
Close to the ground without a sound.
No foot ever fumbles. He never stumbles.
I know he can't talk, but how on earth did he ever
    learn to walk?

Highland Cattle

Oh horned beef!
Cascade of coats!
Head-spread cornucopious!

d b

red   butterfly
fluttered by.

Gilbert's Tortoise, 1780

As soon as Autumn sunlight cools,
Under the heap of mould she goes.
From bonfire night to April Fools
You'll not even see the tip of her nose.

She doesn't give a fig for what she misses,
But snoozes on for half the year.
Without even blinking an eye she hisses
If you so much as dare to tickle her ear.

Much of the summer, too, she sleeps.
She goes to bed at half past four.
Till eleven a.m. she rarely peeps:
Her life is one long boring snore!

But if it turns, as it does, to rain,
She'll not show her sulky face all day.
Drops of rain are all a pain:
Pitter-pat, and she hides away.

She loves warm cloudless summer days
But when the sun is hot – good grief! –
She creeps to find shelter from its rays
Under a shading cabbage leaf.

In Autumn when the sun is feeble
She'll scrabble and tilt herself against a wall:
To keep as warm as possible,
Keels over like a boat in a squall.

But in June she's up and out by six,
Running around as if she's frantic!
She tries to escape, she's full of tricks.
She's in search of a mate. She feels romantic!

Most of her life is a lonely trip:
No trouble or strife – just one long kip!

Frogs' Legs For The Restaurant

Water-weed like a lawn
Laid level on the village-pond

Thousands of periscoping eyes
Peering, blinking, bright

Spies' eyes watching
From thick green hiding

On the bank a boy with a rod
A line and a wicked hook

He casts out the line, far out,
And lays the hook neatly to rest

A leggy nosey disturbance of weed
As frogs crowd round the bait

Then flick, he snatches the line
Up and up, into the air.

Hooked, and legs akimbo,
A frog sails up into the sky

It screams and howls
A terrible human cry

All day the boy stands unmoved
Unmoving: cast, flick and snatch.

He fills a plastic bag:
Frogs' legs for pocket-money.

Missed

He sat with still and watchful care,
Said not a word, but just sat tight.
His net was poised. The fish were there.
'I'll catch one if I do it right.'

He saw a movement in the stream,
Pushed in his widemouthed net, and scraped
The mud which, thick as curdled cream,
Clouded the deeps. And so the fish escaped.

Llook you!

Once in Wales
We saw
A frogogogogoch
Lleaping ofor
A llogogogogoch!

See!

See the salmon
Lleapilng
Up the walterfalll,
Helll-belnt agailnst the fllow!

The Octopuss

The octopuss is a kind of cat,
Four legs in front, and four at the back.
His eyes are as big as tennis-balls
And his mouth makes an O and caterwauls:
'Oh, I works all day beneath the waves,
Scrubbing my doorsteps, washing my caves.
And I gropes and pokes and drags and dredges
For the limpets that cling to the edges of the ledges.
When silly old seabirds come too near
I pounces and wipes away a crocodile-tear,
Then I gulps 'em down, yes I swallows the lot-oh
I washes 'em down with some rum till I'm blotto
Then I curls up and snoozes all night in my grotto.'

Said the Octopus

Said the octopus, after the wedding,
'And what shall we do about bedding?'
'For a bed?' said his wife, 'Use your head!
We can lie on our long legs instead!'

Help!

'Just put the pigs to bed,' said Farmer John,
Going up to bed with his long-johns on.
But, Farmer John, it's easier said than done!
'Cause two are on the roof and won't come down!

Two cheeky pigs are up on the roof
And won't come down!
One is grunt-grunting at the birds,
Wearing a terrible frown!
The other's waylaying silly chickens,
Behaving like a clown!

The rest are grazing, good as gold,
On the green, oh green green grass.
Huffing and puffing, shuffling and snuffling,
Chomping and romping, as they pass.
But two are galumphing on the roof
And I feel such an ass!

If they don't come down soon, I'll be madder
Than the maddest hatter, Farmer John.
So you'd better come and help me. Bring a ladder;
And you'd better keep your long-johns on!

Awakening

Leave this bird-seed
To sleep in the seed-bed,
And see the sparrows
Sprout next Spring.

Cuckoo-spit

Bubbledome
Brightminster
Waterfold
Spittlespital
Airshipshape.

Bird-noise

Scrabblings
Squabblings
Scratchlings
Screechlings
Starlings.

Don Whiskerandos Contrabandista

Don Whiskerandos Contrabandista
Rode into town and captured my sister!

His horse at the gallop, that dashing young blister,
As soon as he saw her, he couldn't resist her.

He twirled his moustaches, he smiled, then he
    kissed her,
Dashed over the mountains and took her to Bicester.

She still sends me postcards, signed, 'Your Loving
    Sister,
Mrs. Whiskerandos Contrabandista.'

For thirty long years now we've all of us missed her,
My whisker-trimming, horse-loving, contraband
    sister!

Waterloo

Napoleon, the roly-poly 'un,
And Skellington, the bony 'un,
Made a great hullabaloo
At the Battle of Waterloo.

They stared at each other
And they shouted rude names.
'I'll go and tell my mother
If you try your old games.'

Bony fired his water-pistol
And stuck out his tongue.
Welly said, 'Watch it! My fist'll
Bop your nose before long.'

They threw bits of bricks
They threw sticks and stones.
Bony said, 'Try any tricks,
And I'll break all your bones.'

Then Welly cried, 'Pax!
There's something in my eye.'
Bony stopped in his tracks.
'Let me help. I can try.'

So they sat down together
And they fixed Welly's eye.
He said, 'I don't know whether
To laugh or cry.'

Then they turned out their pockets –
It was time for a break.
Welly found some biscuits
To go with Bony's bit of cake.

'What shall we do now?'
Said Welly, then frowned.
'Oh, I'm in for a row.
I forgot my paper-round!'

'So what do you all want for your tea?'

'Anything, as long as it's meat,' says Pete.
'With two veg.,' says Reg.
'Lashings of posh nosh,' says Josh.
'Pineapple,' says Dinah. 'Please!'
(Remembering her manners).
'Bacon and peas, and plums from a can,' says Jan.
'Raw carrot,' says the parrot.
'Kate and Sidney,' say Steak and Kidney.
'Yoghurt, a fresh dairy un,'
Says Vic, the vegetarian.
'An egg,' say Meg.
'Make that two,' says Sue.
'Raw carrot,' says the parrot.
'Chocolate cake,' says Jake.
'With boiled ham,' says Pam.
'Half a mo',' says Mom.
'Just listen to me, Pete,
Reg, Josh, Dinah, Kate,
Sidney, Jan, Vic and Meg,
And you, too, Sue.
Here's some money.
Go and get some fish and chips.'
'Raw carrot,' says the parrot.
'Button your lips,' says Mom.

What a Carry-on!

In nineteen hundred and eighty-three
You'll never guess what happened to me!

Dad came shouting up the stairs,
Voice as gruff as any bear's:
'Do the dishes. Feed the cats.
Mind the fire and brush the mats.
Lay the table. Feed the fish.
And your dinner's in the dish.'

By now my Mom was in a state
And shouted, 'Hurry! We'll be late!'
Then Dad grumbled, 'Fuss! Fuss! Fuss!'
And they both ran off to catch the bus.

So I stretched and yawned and then
I went to sleep again.

Fast asleep, I must have dreamed
A funny dream – or so it seemed.
My father whispered, 'Brush the cats!
Feed the dinner. Wash the mats.
Do the table. Eat the dish.
And your fire's in the fish.'

So I scrambled out of bed –
My cheeks were burning, ears bright red –
Put my clothes on, fingers fumbling,
Rushed downstairs, all stumble-tumbling.

Then I blinked and rubbed my eyes.
What a shock! What a surprise!

All the flowers were smiling smiles,
And the broom! Tickling the tiles!
Then the flower-pot laid the table
Quicker than I was ever able.
The watering-can sprinkled the fish
Lying comfy in the dish.
And then the armchair sailed too high
Inviting me to sit, it seemed.

So I sat me down and then it leapt
Into the air and I was swept
Up to the ceiling, round the room,
To the tap-tap of the dancing broom.
And then the armchair sailed too high
And I came tumbling down the sky.
Then, Bang! I landed on the floor
And woke up, feeling bruised and sore.

Then I remembered all those chores
And groaned 'I wish I made the laws!'
I curled up in a heap and then
I simply went to sleep again.

Comparisons

The helicopter-pilot smiled
And twirled his great moustache.
Then up from the helicopter-field
They lifted in a flash.

'It's just like a humming bird,' he said.
'It is!' his passengers nodded.
'Or like a dragonfly,' he said.
'But slightly fatter-bodied.'

'It jumps, it soars, it twists, it twirls,
Its whirring wings spin round.
Up from the earth it whizzes and whirls —
We're a long way from the ground!

'Just like a humming-bird,' they purred.
'Just like a dragonfly!'
'Isn't it marvellous, to fly like a bird,
And watch the clouds go by!'

But when the petrol-tank ran dry
The engine spluttered and stopped.
The helicopter fell through the sky,
And down to earth it dropped.

Into a duckpond it came down — splash! —
The passengers walked under water.
They staggered and shouted: 'That was rash!
You really didn't oughter!'

They pulled the tadpoles out of their hair,
The frogs jumped out of their collars.
The pilot said, 'Come up again. You've paid your
    fare.'
'Not for a million dollars!'

'You said it's like a dragonfly!
It's no such thing!' they spluttered.
'Falling like a stone out of the sky —
Ridiculous!' they muttered.

'You said it's like a humming-bird
That hovers, in the air.
Your comparisons are quite absurd,
Or we'd still be dry, up there!'

A Good View of the Sea

There was an old man who climbed up a tree
Because he wanted to see the sea.

'Before I die, I want to see
The tumbling rumbling sea, you see.'

So he climbed all day up the tallest tree,
And he stubbed a toe and he scrazed a knee.

The people said, 'He'll run out of breath!'
'He'll tumble down!' 'He'll catch his death!'

But when he reached the very top,
He said, 'There's no more tree. I'll have to stop.'

So he lodged himself on a wobbly branch,
Took out his bag, and ate his lunch.

Then he sat for an hour and looked for the sea
But the tide was out and all he could see

Was miles and miles of pebbles and sand:
Not a drop of sea at the edge of the land!

But he said, 'No sweat! I'm in no hurry.'
And soon the sea rushed back with a flurry.

And the waves came crashing on cliffs and in caves,
And sunlight shimmered on a million waves.

And he said as he sat in the top of the tree
'This tree is a wonderful place to be.

'I'll never go down. I'll join the birds.
It's so good up here, I'm lost for words.'

Soon, people came from far and wide
To see him perch on the tree's topside.

They heard him twitter, they heard him coo,
And they threw him food, like at the zoo.

For the rest of his life, he stared at the sea
From the top of the tree, where he wanted to be.

And for the rest of his life he said not a word,
But cooed and twittered and sang like a bird!

Ess'ole

I always liked my grand-dad's house,
With the white fungus in the cellar,
Narrow winding stairs up to the attic,
And the amazing maze of kitchens,
Corridors, sculleries, and sheds.

Until, one day, I cheeked him to his face.
He said quite simply, 'Put the dog out, lad.'
But I was busy exploring a drawer
And said, 'Put it out yourself.'

A moment of shocked silence hung in the air,
And then the old man roared.
He coughed and spluttered, staggered,
And grabbed me by the neck.
His horny nails bit into my flesh.
'Any more lip from you, my lad,
And I'll chuck you into th'ess'ole,'

Meaning the hole for ash beneath the fire,
A hole that glowed bright red like hell,
And seemed to breathe in every draught.

For months, whenever I was bored on rainy days,
And Mother said, 'Go and see your granddad,'
Suddenly, as if by magic, I'd find lots of things to
    do
So that I needn't face the jaws of hell.

Clearing Out

One day my grandfather cleans out
His favourite coat's coat-pockets.

He finds three dusty peppermints
And two electric sockets,
A losing ticket for a raffle
And fifteen paper-clips,
An ointment that works wonders
When the winter cracks your lips,
A broken pen-knife, piles of fluff,
And a crumpled handkerchief,

A packet of seeds, the name rubbed out,
And a carefully pressed leaf
Of his favourite tree, in an envelope
(The leaf, not the tree)
A press-stud and a finger-stall,
And a recipe for mint-tea.

And he says, 'That's funny. Is that all?
I was sure I had some cough-drops.'

So he bangs his coat against the wall,
Filling the house with breezes.
Clouds of dust soon fill the hall,
And tickle his nose till he sneezes.
He beats and shakes, and flaps and flops,
And swings and spins like a top.
Then he splutters, 'Enough!' I'll have to stop!'
And he coughs and coughs until he drops.

Barnet Fair

The night we went to Barnet Fair,
We peeped into the cages there
Rubbed noses with a great brown bear,
Then galloped home on the old gray mare.

The night we went to Barnet Fair
We saw a Thing lurking in its lair.
All it did was lurk and stare
So we all rushed home on the old gray mare.

The night we went to Barnet Fair
It poured with rain and our heads were bare
But we danced and shouted 'We don't care!'
Then we splish-sploshed home on the old gray mare.

The night we went to Barnet Fair
I ate seven sour apples and a mouldy pear.
My stomach groaned and made people stare
So I galloped home on the old gray mare.

The night we went to Barnet Fair
We flew round and round on the Flying Chair
Then we lay on the ground and gasped for air
Till we galloped home on the old gray mare.

The night we went to Barnet Fair
We lost all our pennies on the sideshows there.
Didn't win a thing, shouted – 'It's not fair!'
Then we all galloped home on the old gray mare.

The night we went to Barnet Fair
Candyfloss tangled in our hair
Our toffee apple sticks finished all threadbare
So we all galloped home on the old gray mare.

The night we went to Barnet Fair
We went on the helter-skelter for a scare
Came down backwards for a dare
Then we all staggered home on the old gray mare.

The night we went to Barnet Fair
The dodgems were crowded, not an inch to spare,
And we smashed a car beyond repair,
So we all ran off home on the old gray mare.

The night we went to Barnet Fair
Dick, Dot, and Dave, Kate, Myra and Clare,
Amy, Jim, Matt, and many more were there –
We all rode home on Blossom, the old gray mare.

Tall Story
for Fred Dibnah

Jack Steeplejack,
A joker,
Mended chimbleys
Up North.
One day
The lad
Who worked
For him
Asked for
His cards.
'Why?' said
Jack, sad.
'Going down
Pit,' lad said.
'But why?'
'I'm tired
Of heights,'
Lad said.
Next day
Jack had
New lad
To do chores,
Odd jobs,
Brew tea,
Hod-jobs,
Mix mortar,
Clean bricks,
Push trolley,
Hold brolly
When it rained
Cats and dogs.
Twelve o'clock

Right up
Stack-top
Jack said
To lad,
'Time now
For snap.'
'Oh, I didn't
Bring ought,'
said lad,
Tummy
Rumbling.
'No sweat,'
Jack said.
'You fetch it.
Chish 'n' fips.
Here's a quid.
Be quick.
Mind, now, how
You go.'
Lad clumb
Down ladder,
Five hundred
And eighty-
five rungs.

Walked a
Bit unsteady
To fish shop,
Queued for
Cod 'n' chips.
Climbed up
Five hundred
And eighty-
five rungs.
'Thanks, lad,'
Jack said.

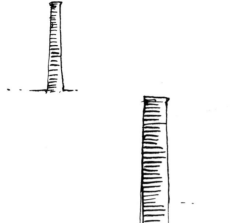

They missed
Vinegar.
Eh?
Whoever
Heard of
Chips
Without?
Eh?'
Lad said,
'Well, I'll
Go and
Get it.'
'No, lad,'
said Jack,
'It's just
My joke.
Eat up
Your snap.
Eh, but
Didn't
You put
Any salt
On, eh?
Better go
And get
Some salt.'

That lad
worked for
Jack for
Twenty years,
Man and boy.
Never did
Know when
Jack was
Joking.

'You're a brick.'
Jack, quick,
Unwrapped
Newspaper.
Then said,
'Where's
Vinegar?'
'Vinegar?'
Said lad,
Out of
Breath.
'Aye, you've
Been had,
My lad.

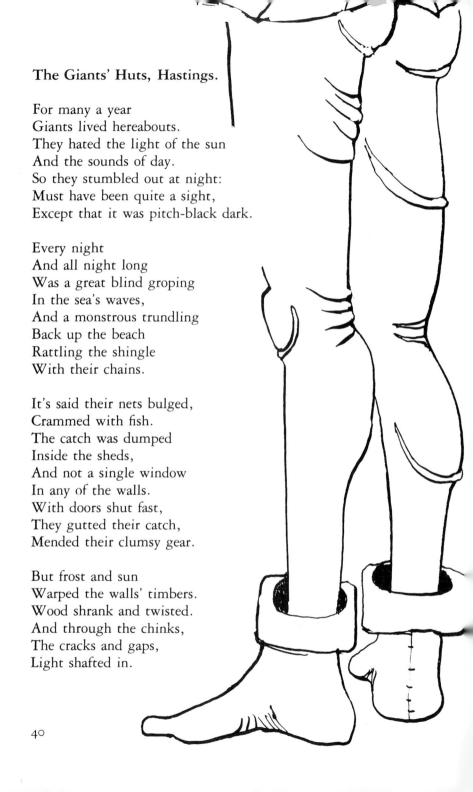

The Giants' Huts, Hastings.

For many a year
Giants lived hereabouts.
They hated the light of the sun
And the sounds of day.
So they stumbled out at night:
Must have been quite a sight,
Except that it was pitch-black dark.

Every night
And all night long
Was a great blind groping
In the sea's waves,
And a monstrous trundling
Back up the beach
Rattling the shingle
With their chains.

It's said their nets bulged,
Crammed with fish.
The catch was dumped
Inside the sheds,
And not a single window
In any of the walls.
With doors shut fast,
They gutted their catch,
Mended their clumsy gear.

But frost and sun
Warped the walls' timbers.
Wood shrank and twisted.
And through the chinks,
The cracks and gaps,
Light shafted in.

40

The man who'd built those sheds
Was long since dead.
No one could be found
To put the sheds to rights.

The shafts of light
Played on the giants' nerves
And one night long ago
They upped and flitted,
Shambled off, groping their way
To distant shady caves.
(They do say you can still
Turn up their bones
If you dig deep enough
In that sea-pounded sand).

They left their last catch to rot:
Billions of bluebottles moved in,
A crazy galaxy
Of blue-enamelled gluttons.
In chorus with the stinking fish
They hummed for weeks,
And left just a heap of gleaming skeletons,
Clean filleted.

That was long 'fore I was born,
And my grandfather, come to that.
Now we all use the sheds
For drying and storing our nets.

But many folks,
When they walk past, at night,
Hurry a bit
And look the other way,
For fear of what they just might see.

Strange Journey

The man who played St. Michael's Church's organ
With all of his ten fingers and two tap-dancing feet —
His name was Johann Sebastian Herbert Morgan —
Once went to the pictures for a special treat,

A four-hour, two-part, science-fiction epic
(With icecream in the intermission)
About a futuristic-prehistoric epoch
And a man named He-man on a special mission.

Next Sunday, during the vicar's boring sermon,
Herbert dozed off in his comfy organ-loft,
Dreamed he was an astronaut named Errman,
Captain of a space-ship that he had to take aloft.

He played the count-down like a hymn-tune,
'O God our help in two, one, zero,'
Aiming his steepled spaceship at the moon,
And pulled the switches, feeling like a hero.

Up, up, and up, the spired space-ship roared,
The altar-candles quivered, stained-glassed windows
  gleamed.
Up and above the clouds brave Errman soared,
The rockets boomed like organ-pipes and Errman
  beamed.

After a day, tired of zoomings, thrusts, and
  spirallings,
He came to rest between two stars, a space
That filled, as if by magic, full of wings!
Angels burst in on Errman, one even slapped his
  face!

'You're late, you're late, a thousand years late!'
They shouted in a terrifying tizz,
'Your timetable must be years out of date!
We've been waiting for this bus five centuries!'

They nagged him till his nerves began to teeter.
They thumped him with their flashing bristly wings.
They threatened to report him to St Peter,
And told him to get a proper grip on things!

'But where exactly do you want to go?'
Poor Errman asked them, feeling his courage fail.
'Where do we want to go? But don't you know?
Why, down to earth, you idiot! Go! Set sail!'

'All aboard!' poor Errman cried. 'Hold tight!'
And pressed the buttons, one, two, three.
Soon all the space in space was out of sight,
And plonk he landed in a churchyard tree.

'Amen!' the vicar said. 'Amen' again, and coughed.
Poor Herbert shook himself out of his dream.
'Amen!' a thousand angels sang aloft,
And Herbert played 'Time like an ever rolling
    stream.'

Whenever Herbert Morgan looks at the tall church
    spire
Or starts dozing off in the vicar's dreary drone,
He pinches himself, and feels his hands perspire,
And when the stained glass angels smile, he moans a
    little moan.

A Grand Obsession
For Rosemary Lee

Grandma said, with a nod of her head,
'As sure as one and one make two,
I'll go and see the Grand Canyon
If it's the last thing I do!'

So every day for years
She saved all her cash,
Sometimes frowned and shook her head:
'I think I'm being very rash.'

Once a month she wondered,
But that grand hole in the ground
Sat tight inside her head
All the year round.

Finally she'd saved enough
And went and paid her fare.
Put piles of cash on the counter,
And said, 'Now I'll soon be there!'

Slowly she packed her bags.
'Shall I take this coat or that?
Does it ever rain in Arizona?
Shall I need to take a hat?'

A Jumbo took her to Los Angeles,
An elephant with wings;
She saw millions of cars like performing fleas
Going round and round in rings.

She went to look at the film stars' homes,
To peep and poke her nose.

But all she saw was fences and walls
And a gardener with a hose.

Then round Las Vegas's neon streets
She took a daring ramble,
Saw elastic acrobats cabaret
And decided not to gamble.

Then she took the coach to the Canyon,
Her eyes nearly popped out of her head.
The sunset glowed on redstone cliffs.
'It's even better than they said!'

Next morning, bright and early,
Almost before first light,
She went to the local airfield
And asked to take a flight.

A young pilot said he'd take her
And show her all the sights.
'But your plane's so very small!' she said.
'Is it big enough for flights?'

The pilot held up his finger.
'The wind's not too strong,' he said.
So they clambered aboard and took off,
And she thought, 'I'll soon be dead.'

He flew straight into the Canyon,
And tipped the plane on its side.
'You've never seen anything like this!' he said.
'Are you enjoying the ride?'

Her stomach went quite crazy.
The blood rushed to her head.
Her vision went blurred and hazy.
'It's very interesting,' she said.

Soon she got used to the flying,
And sat back snug in her seat.
Saw great rocks, and the river winding
Like a ribbon beneath her feet. . . .

A week later we met her at the airport,
Safe and sound, back on land.
'How'd you like the Grand Canyon?' we asked her.
'The Grand Canyon? Oh, it was grand!'

Mind Your Step

Up to the top of the old castle-tower
Bill and his father climbed the spiral-stair.
Five minutes felt more like half an hour,
And when they reached the top they had no breath
    to spare.

Their eyes were level with the high church-steeple,
The weather-cock stared them in the eye.
The ants crawling below were really people,
And Bill seemed to be standing in the sky.

'Time we were off. We mustn't be late,'
His father said. 'You go down first.
The stairs are dangerous, so hold on tight
And just mind where you put your feet.'

Bill took the smooth steps one by one.
His father came behind him, very close.
'Now mind that step. It's badly worn.
You'll fall if you don't follow your nose.'

Bill felt his father breathing down his neck.
'Now watch your feet. You're going to trip.'
His dad's knees nudged him in the back,
And heavy toe-caps poked him on the hip.

And then his father fell down – smack! –
His legs collapsed, all over the place.
He grabbed for the rail, and wrenched his back.
Anger and pain screwed up his face.

'Now see what you've made me do!
Why can't you be sensible, do as you're told?
I don't know what's got into you!
And fasten your coat, before you catch cold!'

Washday Battles

On washday in the good old bad old days
Before the launderette, machine and drier,
My mother used to use her own bare hands,
A posher, mangle, line, a wooden horse and fire.

At dawn she blew small coals into a blaze
Under well-water in a brim-full copper.
Soon as the water seethed and steamed into a haze
The clothes were seized. They plunged, and came a
    cropper.

Submerged, they scalded, lunged and tossed,
Squelched by fire-water through and through,
Until she gripped her soggy wooden stick
And levered them, steaming, out, all black and
    blue,

Carried them, soggy and limply dripping,
Chucked them onto the washboard-tub,
Where she set to, and thumped and slapped
And poshed and punched them, rub-a-dub.

Then she grabbed each punch-drunk one in turn
Wrung its neck, squeezed all its juice outright.
Corkscrewed and throttled, flat out it lay, quite
   dead,
And then she set to again, and beat it white.

Straightway she fed it to the lion-roaring mangle,
Into tight-rolling rubber lips, which sucked it in
Then slurped it out again, pancaked
To a wafer, breathless, depressed, and thin.

And then she flung them over her arm,
Hauled them out to the windy backyard plot,
Shook them out, cracked them like a whip,
Then strung them up and hanged the lot.

Soon as the wind possessed those wretched shapes,
Their arms would wildly wave, their legs kick free,
The skirts would billow out, voluminous,
And all the washing blew out, flew out, on the
    spree.

Mimicking Nelson's flags (England expects . . .)
They semaphored 'A Terrible To-do!'
'Clothes Saved From Drowning.' 'All Hands Saved!'
'Housewife Fails Again To Drown This Gallant
    Crew!'

A Yorkshire Tale

See that road crawling up the side of that great hill?
The road that winds under the Whitestone Cliff,
    they call it.
See how steep it is? And how it twists and turns?
Awkward for buses, even grinding up in bottom
    gear.
Cyclists generally go the long way round, avoiding
    it,
And so do lorries, if the drivers have any gumption.

Now, years ago, great teams of horses, six or eight,
Dragged waggons up that road, right to the very
    top.
And the man in charge always gripped the brake,
Ready to slam it on, to stop the waggon rolling
    back,
Whenever the horses failed or lost their grip,
Rolling back, and dragging both men and horses
    down,
Crashing back down the hill. . .

Before the days of lorries and such newfangled
    things,
I used to watch those waggons creaking up . . .
The teams of horses pulling and straining at the
    chains,
Leaning heavy into their bursting collars,
Digging their iron shoes into the ruts to get a hold,
All froth and slaver round their mouths and bits,
And bathed in sweat all over, top to toe.

And worst of all was Gormire Lake.
Folks always reckoned it has no bottom,
And I won't argue either way.
Roll backwards down that hill, and sure as –
Sure as eggs have shells on,
You'll end up, black and blue, in Gormire Lake.
They say that once a waggon and team –
The best, the beautifullest black beasts for miles
　　around –
Missed their step, and the brakes all failed.

One poor fellow, when he saw the waggon start to
　　slide,
Rushed to get a chain slung round the wheels,
And was smashed to smithereens for his trouble.
And the great waggon thundered every inch,
Right down, crashing to the brink of Gormire Lake.
The waggon went plunging in, and dragged the
　　horses
With it, thrashing black water into froth,
A frenzy of wheels and legs and crazy eyes.
And never seen again, not a trace.
The waggon, the load, the team, all gone,
Completely disappeared. Or so they say
And to my dying day, I'll never forget
The thrill of terror and hope I used to feel
When I was a kid, watching some team
Of sweating horses dragging their waggon
And its load up Whitestone Cliff.
I half wanted them to slip and slide
And lose their footing, and come crashing down,
Go somersaulting into Gormire Lake,
To see if that story was true;
But my other half – the better half,
I like to think – prayed that they'd make the top,
To rest and drink and live to pull another day.

1945

The news was of inhumanity,
Of crimes, obscenities,
Unspeakable insanity
And bestial atrocities.

Somebody turned the radio down.
Nobody said a word.
Auschwitz, Buchenwald, and Belsen:
'It couldn't happen here,' they said.

At school the teacher set revision:
Of the princes murdered in the tower,
The Spanish Inquisition,
And Genghis Khan drunk with power;

Of heretics, burnt at the stake,
Refusing to deny a vow;
Mass-murders for religion's sake;
He said, 'It couldn't happen now.'

'You're next,' the school-bullies snigger,
'Don't try any silly tricks!'
All through History he tries to figure
A way out of punches and kicks.

At the end of morning-school,
They drag him to an air-raid shelter.
Down into darkness, damp and cool,
With Puncher and Kicker and Belter.

They tear off all his clothes
And tread them on the floor.
With obscenities and oaths,
They let him have what-for.

Their tortures are very crude,
Clumsy and unrefined.
With a sudden change of mood
They pretend to be friendly and kind.

They change their tack once more
And punch him black and blue.
He ends, crouched on the floor,
And finally they're through.

With a special parting kick
They warn him not to talk.
He feels wretched, sore and sick,
Gets up, can hardly walk.

It's a beautiful Summer day,
His eyes squint in the sun.
He hears two passing women say,
'Oh, schooldays are such fun.'

Words echo in his head:
'Couldn't happen here,' they said.
And 'Couldn't happen now,' they said.
He never breathes a word.

The Old Canal

On the stillest of still days
We lay on the towpath to look
Down into clear depths.
We saw ourselves looking up, drowned.
We tapped the water with finger-tips
And our faces wobbled like jelly.
Tapped again and they broke up.

Under the bridge, cool and dark:
Light bounced off deep water
To play on the bridging vault
Of curving brick: a ghostly
Play of wavy trembling light,
Oscillating, oscillating.

Every day, the dare:
To cross the bridge, outside the wall.
A bare toe-hold on the lip of bricks.
Clung to the parapet, arms outstretched,
Fingers aching, scratching a hold.
Reached safety, trembling.

Near factories, canal-water
Always a rusty red soup,
Stinking of bitter iron.
We threw sticks: 'Fetch it, boy!'
He did, and stank to high heaven
For at least a week.
'Stay outside, pongy dog!'

Old sacks, stacked with bricks,
Took dead dogs to the bottom,
Lay in deep mud, disintegrated.
The corpses rose, ballooned,
The colours of death.

In clear stretches, stickle-
Backs, big-eyed, flickery.
We netted them, scraped off
The limpets, little plates
Like cancers: gristley
Grizzled and grisley.

Water-boatmen, long-legged,

Balanced on dimples of water,
Performing their ordinary miracle.

Dragon-flies, encased in enamel,
Decorated the flags with their pennants.

Beetles, shoe-black shiny,
Shot up like rockets,
Surfaced, gulped air,
Then down again
Like suicidal dive-bombers.

Best of all, the barge-horses,
Thudding, treading
For purchase, straining
Shouldering, muscles at a stretch.

Ropes of grassy saliva
Hung, swinging.
And the barge, dark as night,
Looming like a giant coffin.
Always at the stern, silent,
A man or woman at the tiller,
Dark and silent as an undertaker.

Worst of all, my brother getting lost.
We searched the towpaths, bridges.
Was he already under water?
At ten, he couldn't swim,
Was crazy about canals.

At nightfall, he was still not found.
Fears bubbled up
Inside our minds,
Like the frantic gurgling
Of a drowning boy.

His face was in my mind's eye,
White, silent, staring from eyes
Now blind, wide open, dead.

When he came strolling home,
A torrent of questions.
'What's all the fuss about?'
He asked. He'd found
A new exciting friend
With an even more exciting
Even newer model railway.
Shunting, moving signals,
Changing points,
They'd lost all track of time.

He was sent upstairs.
Then thrashed.
There was a sudden rush
Of sheer vexation,
The sharp anger of relief.

For months, every night,
Falling asleep, I saw
His drowning face.

Strange Exchange

In the middle of the night one night
I woke to hear a neighbour's horse,
Caught up in some nightmarish fright,
Screech owlishly till well nigh hoarse.
And then an owl in the nearby spinney
Began to snigger, neigh, and whinny,
For what seemed half the night, without a pause.

In dark and deepest sympathy
They played their moonlight symphony
Of scream and hoot and howl.
The owl with the horse's snicker,
And the horse with the voice of the owl.

And as I lay there sleeplessly, I thought,
Sooner than be bewildered by this crazy pair,
I'd rather be deep in sleep and caught
In the tangled web of my favourite nightmare.

A Warning Not to Walk
On the Moors at Night

'Jack o' the Lantern,
Jack o' the Light,
Jack in the quagmire,
Every night.'

Will o' the Wisp,
Will o' the Flame,
Nightly plays
His gruesome game.

Lures lone walker,
Wandering late,
Deep into danger,
Fearsome fate.

He slips on stone,
And slides in mire,
Following gleams
Of fairy fire.

Flibbertigibbet
Rides the air,
Flabbergasts
The traveller.

Fools his feet,
Hoaxes his eyes,
Shocks him, shakes him,
Dread surprise.

Slips and staggers,
Tumbles in,
Up to the neck,
Up to the chin.

Whistling winds,
Hooting owl,
Hungry wolves
On the prowl.

Hackles bristle,
Nostrils flare,
Smell of death
Is on the air.

Screeching cats
Hunt apace,
Skittering bats
Brush his face.

Clouds go scudding   At midnight hour
In cold skies,   He goes astray
Moonlight glares   Left to flounder
On staring eyes.   Till break of day.

Rumblings and Grumblings

'Where's the lad that's hiding in my house?'
Grumbled the giant, hurling chairs about.
'I'll find him, even if he's quiet as a mouse,
And eat him in one gulp. There's no way out!'

He stomped and roared, and thumped and banged,
Until he'd smashed the furniture, and then
He poked about the fireplace. 'I'll be danged!
He's got out, up the chimney. Foiled again!'

'Where's the girl that's hiding in my house?'
Croaked the old witch, giving her cat a nudge.
'Good for nothing moggy! Couldn't catch a mouse!'
Felix agreed, and mewed, 'I don't intend to budge.'

She rushed about the house, as light as any bird,
Searched high and low, and even poked the cinders.
And then the curtains softly stirred;
'Drat it!' she croaked. 'I forgot to close the
    windows.'

Lurker

         The old man lurked behind a tree.
School was over, I was free.
I ran, jumped, shouted 'Cheerio'
And found some pebbles to kick and throw.
         The old man lurked behind a tree.
I went to the park to chase the birds.
I chased them all, well at least two thirds.
I went on the slide. I had a swing.
And then I stopped. I'd done everything.
         The old man lurked behind a tree.

I started for home. It was time for tea.
And my favourite programme on T.V.
I was hungry now. My tummy rumbled.
I kicked a stone. And then I stumbled.
         The old man lurked behind a tree.
'Do you want a sweet?' he said, soft and mild.
He held it out. I paused. He smiled.
Not a sound. It was getting late.
I was the fish. The sweet was the bait.
         The old man lurked behind the tree.

'Here have a sweet. Come on. It's free.'
And then I minded what Mother had said:
'If a stranger stops you, just keep your head.
If it's a man, say, "You're not my Dad."
He'll understand, if he's O.K.
In any case, just run away.'

So I kept my head. In fact, I shook it.
And that tempting sweet, I never took it.
'You're not my Dad!' I said. 'No way!'
And then I turned and ran away.
I looked back twice and I could see
         The old man still lurking behind the tree.

Dusk-Change

Cats turn into tigers
Swallows into bats
Trees turn into witches
Harmless mice to rats.

Eyes turn into stares
Sun into pale moon
Dreams turn into nightmares
And 'Never!' into 'Soon!'

Streams turn into chuckles
Rivers into roars
Windows turn to glancing eyes
And pigs into wild boars.

Winds turn into shrieking
Pigeons into owls
Butterflies to fluttering moths
And barking dogs to howls.

Day turns into night
Awake falls asleep,
So let's all hope for slumber,
Untroubled, still, and deep.

Night-Visit

We stood outside in the last of the light,
Waiting to hear it,
Hoping for a sight.
But would it come?

We heard a car make a distant purr,
A rustle of leaves,
A wisp astir.
But would it come?

We tensed our ears till they almost popped.
A bat flittered close.
Our breathing stopped.
But would it come?

Staring at the sky made our eyeballs ache
But we kept on the watch
For our visitor's sake.
Would it ever come?

Suddenly it burst across the darkening sky
With a rasping croak
And a high-pitched cry!
Yes, it had come!

With a whirr of wings it stroked the dark
Squeaking shrill
Through its throaty bark.
Yes, it had come!

With its long pointing beak it probed the night
Tracing a line
Between dark and light.
Just in time.

Nightly it ranged the thickening air
Circled the woods
Then back to its lair,
Its secret home.

Riding the last gray trace of light,
Reading the shadows,
Roding into night,
In a nick of time.

Nightly the woodcock staked its claim,
Taking its place,
Speaking its name.
For this it came.

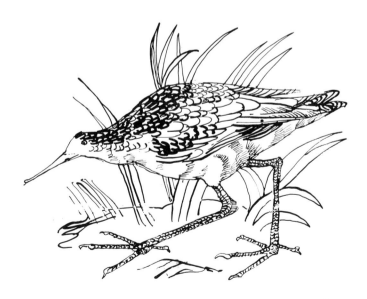

Dare

'Rawhead and Bloody Bones
Steals naughty children from their homes,
Takes them to his dirty den
And they are never seen again.'

He lurks at the bottom of the pit
Staring with one bloodshot eye,
Wallows in the sludge and slime,
Tempts us to venture close and pry.

We crawl right up to the very edge,
Peer into dripping pitch-dark mine.
Our fingers cling tight to the ledge
And shudders riot down my spine.

'Come out, old Rawhead, Bloody Bones!'
We heckle and bawl into the pit.
'Head!' 'Bones!' come echoing back,
Then, bolder still, we crouch and spit.

'Gob in your eye, old Bogeyman!'
We gather a heap of bricks and stones
And fling them fast and furious,
Hoping to hear his wounded groans.

Then, scattering to confuse his speed, –
Vamoose! – we run for dear life.
Our hackles rise, our ears burn,
His breath comes sharp as a butcher's knife.

Winded and shaken, we all flop down,
Giggling with terror and delight.
The cheerful sky fills our eyes,
And we bathe in a comforting sea of light.

Samurai's Kendo

armadilloshouldered
crocodilearmoured
swordedgeswifter
    thansound
maskofterrorvisored
poisedalertontiptoe
mailglovedhands
    largerthanlife
holdingdeathready
    forthefatalblow
serenethefaceinshadow
unspeakingthetautmouth
watchfulthesteady
    eyesunblinking
impenetrablethesuit
    withoutachink
tremblingwecontemplate
perfectioninyouract
supremacyinyourinaction
whenwillyoumovetostrike?
comesoonandstrikewepray
thecleanexecutionof
    yoursword
proclaimingdeathaccomplished
theshortflightofyourterrible
    sword
thatwillbesomesortofmercy
afterintolerablesuspense
    ofsilence
    ofyoursteelysilence
    strikenow
    strikenow
    strikestrike
andsowewishourselvestodeath.

No Cure

Carroty-haired, freckle-face bag of bone,
At eight she went to hospital alone.

Doctors worked on her body, and they put it right.
But heart-ache hurt her hard, alone at night.

She called out to the nurse, she cried her name.
She called persistently, but no-one came.

She scrambled from her bed, confused, perplexed,
Crept from the ward, felt lost, and asked, 'Where
    next?'

Wrapped in her blanket, on the floor she curled,
All through the bleakest hour of the turning world.

She peered into the shadows round about
And suddenly shocked the darkness with a shout.

'God, let me out!' she cried, then held her breath.
A nurse came fast. 'Good gracious, child! You'll
    catch your death.

And what exactly are you doing out of bed?
Sensible girls all settle down when they've been fed.'

'But I've got an ache,' she said. 'I've got a pain.'
'Your tummy is it?' nurse enquired. 'And has it
    come again?'

'No, it's my heart,' she said, 'my heart is sore.'
'Ah, we have no cure for that,' said nurse, lifting
    her body from the floor.

Billy The Dare

Billy Buggins, scrap-dealer, scrounger,
Had a bristling Desperate-Dan chin,
And a foghorn voice that bulled and boomed
Out of a deep dark broken cave.

We dared each other to tag onto his heels,
And taunt and tease with cheek.
With canny startling speed, he'd drop his load
And chase us down the street, eyes rolling wild.

His teeth gnashed like the rasp of a saw,
Hobnailed boots pounded and crashed and scraped.
You'd swear his breath was hot on your neck,
His clawing grimy fingers snatching at your neck.

And suddenly he'd stop and stand and sway.
He'd slap his knee, guffaw with glee,
Sweep bottles of milk from someone's step
And gulp a pint or two to slake his terrible thirst.

Winter's Night

Psst! Yes, you! Why don't you come inside?
You don't want to? But you'll catch your death!
I promise, I don't intend to take you for a ride.
Look! It's so cold I can even see your breath.

I know we don't know you, but that's no reason.
Just come in and get warm. You look perished.
And you tell me – is winter time the season
For sleeping under stars? And I bet you're famished.

It's no trouble at all, you can have the spare bed.
Now, I'm going to have to close this back-door
    soon,
But I don't want you to wake up dead.
How can you just lie there under the freezing moon?

So – what's that you say? Your name's Jack Frost?
Well, why on earth didn't you say so, first?

Nightmares

1. Typewrither

Forty-three quick
Metal tentacles
Caged on the table;
See them fly up,
Plucking at the paper.

2. Weird Noises in my Head

The thunder of camelry charging into bottle
To the music of drummerdary and magpiper
Made my blood curl and my hair curdle.

Reading A Bonfire, Top to Bottom.

Sparks expire just as they meet the stars.
Smoke thins out, dissolved in air.
Fingers of smoke in sparkling gloves reach up.
Smoke as thick as wrists wrestles into darkness.
Tips of flame singe late-wandering insects.
Great fists of flame punch bales of smoke into the
   sky.
Guy's hat has tilted and burns like hair.
The face is a bubbling horror-mask.
Buttons are popping off like fireworks.
He wears a coat of flame and ruin.
The rest of him has sunk into the furnace.
Here the heart's so hot, to look would burn your
   eyes.
Chestnuts and baked potatoes sweat and crack.
Already ash is piling up like white-hot snow.
The grass that grew here will be slow to come again,
Tomorrow all we'll know is a patch of scorched
   earth.

Bonfire Night Snapshots

His mind gripped
The rocket as his hands
Released it.
He rose two hundred feet,
Riding the cardboard tube,
And turned so giddy
He fell down.

Too late, their mother
Rushed out to search
And in the ashes
She found the handles
Of the drawers
Of her best old wardrobe.

The Sublime and the Gorblimey

I

Great cyclists in a fierce race,
Like the epic Tour de France,
Move their wheels with perfect pace
And the rhythms of a dance.

Bicycle and rider –
Everything fuses,
Nothing refuses.

When things go really well,
They know, but can't tell,
The amazing magic spell
That seems to propel
Them like bats out of hell!

Bike and rider
Move as one,
In perfect unison,
Of frame and skeleton.

2

When I go cycling for a day,
The same sorts of things occur,
In a way, well sort of, you might say.
At first, wheels smoothly purr
And the rush of the road
Is a thrill.
But after a mile or two
Of long hard slogs up hills,
My cycle gets to be all thumbs,
And awkward collapsible legs,
And flailing arms and blistered bums.
It even sits up and begs,
And is specially good at spills.

It's no longer a bike, but a tyke, or a moke, or a
    joke,
All twisted chain, and pain, and strain. A real
    drain.

Enough of this talk.
I'm going for a walk.

Pizzeria Blues

My brother loves Salami
But she just thinks he's barmy.
He tries to catch her ear
In her noisy pizzeria
But every time he meets her
He blushes when he greets her
And he falls into a stammer
and his heart beats like a hammer
In The Leaning Tower of Pizza.

Sal, she doesn't give a fig.
'I've got lots of boys! You dig?
Some real muscular and big.'
She hoots and does a jig.
Yes, her boys are really neat, sir
In the leaning tower of pizza.

I say, 'Brother, are you crazy?
Why not Mary, Jane or Maisy?
Or Jemima, June, or Daisy?
Sal's a tearaway, a teaser,
Dodgy as the tower of Pisa.
You can never hope to please her.'

But my brother loves Salami.
I say, 'Go and join the army.'
But his face goes soft and smarmy
And he blurts, 'I love Salami.'
So I say, 'Oh boy, you're barmy.'

'Your insults never harm me,'
Says my brother. 'Ah! Salami!
How that girl can charm me!'

Tap-Dancing
for Liberty Blake

Antics in the attics,
Antics in the cellars,
Upstairs and downstairs,
Tap-dancing fellahs!

Bill Bojangles, Buck and Bubbles,
Tap your way through all your troubles!
Bunny and Sandman, Chuckles and Chuck,
Dance your way through all kinds of luck!

Tap your toes and tap your heels,
Let us know how the tapdancer feels!
Tiptop in the morning, toptoe at night,
Tap toes and heels till we all come out right!

Tap to your funeral, tap into the ground,
Tap up to heaven and look around!
Tap Saint Peter and his bunch of keys,
Tap Old Gabriel if you please!
Tap toe and heel every cloud-capped tower
Tap every cloud till it runs a shower!
Tap the old sun for solar power
Tap it to the earth, open every flower!
Tap in the thunder and tap in the rain
Tap till the whole world rings again!

One two, three four five,
Tap again till you feel alive!
Six, seven, eight nine ten,
Tap for all you're worth, then tap again!
Seven, eight, nine ten eleven,
Tap for the earth and tap for heaven!

Sailors' Hornpipe

Let us splash our cash
In the market-place tonight.
Come and have a bash
And we'll set the town alight —
We'll have
Roasted taters,
Fried tomaters,
Jellied eels,
A dish of spinach,
Whelks, shirimps
With vinegar,
And chish and fips.
Then we'll dance a jig and all work up a raging
   thirst
And we'll tope and swig and booze and caper! Who
   goes first?

Let's drink
Lemonade
And brandy
Lime and porter
And a shandy
And Jamaican rum
And cider punch
Until we burst.

Let us punch and fight,
Lay about us till we fall,
Pinch and poke and smite,
Bang the blighters on the wall!
Pull a muscle,
Scrimmage, scuffle
Pull his ear off in the tussle,

Let's all wrangle,
Jostle, bustle,
In a bar-room brawl!

When the rozzers come to grab and drag us to the
    nick,
We'll go flying through the window like a flick-
    knife — flick!
And skedaddle
Out of trouble
Like greased lightning,
Slip the cable,
Belt off double quick
Before their flipping handcuffs click.

Through Four Holes

Through the holes in this cheese
I can see you looking at me.
You are going to say,
'Stop playing with the cheese
And get on with your food.
I shan't tell you again!'

Through the hole in this fence
I can see the trees in the wood
Where Trespassers Will Be Prosecuted.
Can they prosecute my eyeball?

Through the hole in this toast
The butter has dribbled down
Onto the clean table-cloth.
If I move this plate, they won't notice.

Through the hole in my trouser pocket
I poked one finger, then another.
Now, there's no pocket left.
Just a hole, as big as my fist.

Place-Names

Do goblins still lurk in their secret lair
At Pucklechurch and Puckeridge?
Do mouse-hawks soar on the rising air
High over Pudleston bridge?

At Fletchamstead do the bacons smoke
Until they're cured just right?
And at Foxton and Foxley do sensible folk
Still lock up their sheep at night?

At Dunnockshaw are the hedgerows bright
With the hedgesparrows' cheerful song?
Are the ditches in Galby town still white
With the bone of one who did wrong?

At Appleshaw do the trees in the park
Bear so much fruit that they sag?
Do folk still fear to walk after dark
On the slopes of Wolfhole Crag?

Oddservations

The cricks in Wimbledon necks
Make a terrible racket.

The neat boxer
Made a nice packet.

'Every day, the rush-hour
Is poke-and-push-hour,'
The bus-conductor thundered.

'My passengers shoot
Straight in and out.
Never pay. Never stay.
Why ever not?'
The lightning-conductor wondered.

From his fold
Jack Shepherd sold
A ewe to me
For tuppence.

St. Patrick unravels
Dangers of Irish travels:
In towns dogs bark.
In country bog's dark.

Time to go:
Jumbo
Packs his trunk.

Homesick
Sad kangaroo
In London Zoo
Is out of bounds.

Blurred by the rain
On the windscreen:
Ollotrunk or elethump!

A Jumbo-sized thirst:
He trank and trank and trank
Up and up and up his nose,
Restocking his hose.

Revenges:
1.
When he hit the bull's eye
The bull just hit him back.

2.
'This,' said the sturgeon,
'Is a special treat:
Best-quality human meat,
Cut from an eminent surgeon.'

Old Windbag came shuffling down the road,
When we were all at play.
He talked and talked and talked so loud
He blew us all away.

In the enchanted castle
We were dazzled
By light bewitched:
Candelabracadabra.

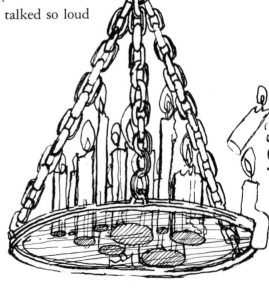

Nowhere

Is where they pay you
To travel on the train
And when you slurp your orange juice
There's no-one to complain.

Where important people beg you
To travel free on the bus
And when you spill your icecream
Nobody makes a fuss.

Park keepers say, 'Walk on the Grass.'
'Take a deckchair. There's no fee.'
And O.A.P.'s don't need a pass,
For everything is free.

The dustmen drive Rolls Royces,
All fully automatic,
Delivering marvellous rubbish
For everybody's attic.

The firemen in winter
Drive for miles and miles
To light a bonfire for you
With chuckles and cheerful smiles.

The telephones ring with laughter,
And feed you sausage rolls,
While brilliant leaves and flowers
Sprout from the telegraph poles.

Words in a Cage

The words in the cage
Made very small sounds
Pick Peck Tip Tap
Zip Zoo Seed Sad
Hip Hop and Hope

When they tried to move —
Flight Flutter Flagitate —
They flew into the bars
And just fell back.

One day we opened the cage
And they all flew out.
What a hullabaloo!
They exploded into song —
A carolling chorus:

Flamboyant Flamfleur!
Flavescent Flageolet!
Flawless Fluctuation!
Flarepath Flammation!

And as they all flew
Up into the sky
Their parting word
Fell about our ears:
Floccinaucinihilipilification!

Floccinaucinihilipilification

Hot and Cold

October, November, December,
Glow, like an ember,
Roast, warm as toast,
Heat your feets, under the sheets.

January, February, March,
Freeze, stiff as starch,
Flakes blow, cheeks glow,
Feet trudge slow, through the snow.

The calendar of my year

JABUARY	FEVERARY	MARSH
HAYDRILL	PERHAPS	SOON
DEW LIE	HAW GUST	SOFT UMBER
OCTOBURR	NEW EMBER	DISMEMBER

Delayed Action

In the Big February Freeze-Up
I went skating – well, sliding – on the lake.
I did a bottoms-down-and-knees-up
But the cold was intense and made my face ache.

Ice-drops clustered on my nose
And I seemed to lose my voice.
My shouts and yells all gelled and froze
Into lumps of ice.

In the Great March Thaw
I went to watch the ice break
And heard my shouts of a month before
Resounding over the lake.

I stood and listened to my own voice
And heard it proclaim a host
Of 'Oohs!' and 'Ahs!' I had no choice
But to stand and listen to my own ghost!

All – Fours

Come and leaf through the lawn
Over and over, over and over
Uncover, discover, re-cover
A leafleafleafleaf clover.

Enter the Spiders

Barleybrown oatlight legs
Come pattering in,
Autumn rainday guests
In their harvest bests.

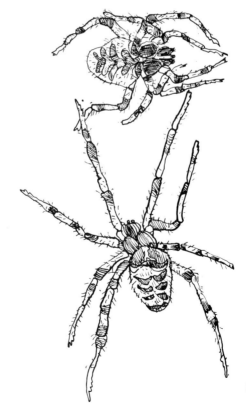

Sci-fi Horrorscopes

1. At Martian dawn
   In fireproof boots
   Trepid explorers
   Pussy-foot
   Round the lip
   Of the mouth
   Of the tepid volcano,
   Hoping it won't wake up
   And yawn.

2. Proudly he stepped out
   Out onto the new planet
   And his booted foot
   Dissolved.

3. Like a sharp attack of fear,
   The dexterous control-column
   Gripped his stomach.

4. 'Come back inside!'
I yelled to my twin.
But she was snatched up
By the rubber midwife.

5. As I went to shake him by the hand –
Congratulations, a successful mission –
It turned to jelly.

6. 'Are you there?'
'Where?'
'Down there!'
'I am.'
'Who are you?'
'I've no idea!'

7. Fumbling desperately, madly,
Finally he managed to jerk his knife
From its protective scabbard
And gasped to see it neatly slice
Through his oxygen-pipe.

8. Every night and all night
Earthly nightmares
Mar Mars.

9. One, two,
   Buckle my toe.
   Three, four,
   It fitted before.
   Five, six,
   You're in a fix.
   Seven, eight,
   What a fate!
   Nine, ten:
   To have to learn to walk again!

10. If only I could walk, or even crawl,
    I could get some food from the ship.
    Then I could have a meal,
    If only Ed hadn't borrowed my stomach.

11. 'What can you see through the telescope?'
    'Red rivers crossing a white landscape.'
    'So his eyes are very bloodshot.
    He's old, so we may escape!'

12. 'Why bring all that junk into the ship?
You know it's very crowded!'
'But I want to bring some souvenirs
Of dear old Mother Earth.'
'But why on earth – why, in heaven's name?'
'Because I enjoyed my time there.
Besides, it's being demolished next week.'

Tomorrow

A dazzling yellow thunderbolt whizzes through the
 rain —
A flash of bright blue lightning —
It's the High Speed Train.

Wave on Tuesday morning to the Scots in old
 Dunblane,
Rush back to York for Monday night
On the High Speed Train.

Buy a cup of tea at Euston, finish it in Spain,
Fly right over Biscay
In the High Speed Train.

Travel fast in comfort, not a hint of pain,
Leave your aching head behind,
On the High Speed Train.

Shoot across the Forth Bridge, quick as water down
 a drain,
No time to see the water
On the High Speed Train.

No more of late arrivals, we'll never more complain —
If all the parts are working
On the High Speed Train!

Railway Museum Headphones

Stephenson's smoking Rocket
Rattled. 'Pocka, pocka, pocket.'

Puffing Billy puffed when the track was hilly:
'Puffer, puffer, puff.' It sounded quite silly.

'Diddly dah, diddly dah,' the old steam engine said,
Then they put it to bed in the old-engine shed.

When The Flying Scotsman blew its whistle
It sounded like wild bagpipes stung by a thistle.

When the newfangled electric lights in Queen
    Victoria's special royal deluxe carriage fused,
She said, 'We are not amused.'

It's Ned!

I said, 'This book, sir, will you read?'
And soon the book was read.
I said, 'This loaf, sir, will you knead?'
And soon the loaf was kned.

I said, 'This dog, sir, will you feed?'
And soon the dog was fed.
I said, 'This book, sir, do you need?'
'Oh yes,' he said, 'it's ned.'

Economy

The words in this book were made entirely from
    recycled letters.
They've all been used before by my elders and
    betters.
Unpack them now, and stack them on your shelf.
Then, when you need them, you can use them
    yourself.

Good Night!

That's not the right time, is it?
Midnight? You'd better be off.
I must say, I enjoyed your visit.
But I hope you've not caught my cough.

Good night! Mind how you go!
Wrap up warm against the frost.
Mind how you cycle through the snow.
Go carefully, and don't get lost!

Well, I'll be — look, they've drained the bottle!
Nothing to do now but hit the sack till
Noon. Then look for a rhyme for axolotl,
And for that tricky blighter, pterodactyl.